# THE 100 YEAR TIME TRAVELERS

# THE 100 YEAR TIME TRAVELERS

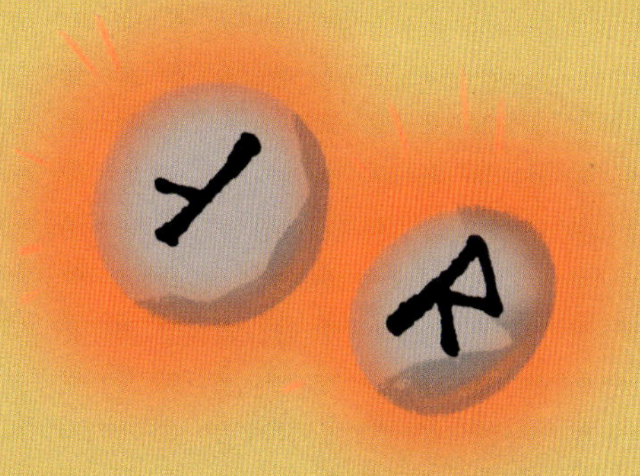

Illustrated by Adrienne Green
Written by Philip Steele

weldonowen

**Written by Philip Steele**
**Illustrated by Adrienne Green**

weldon**owen**


Published by Weldon Owen Children's Books
An imprint of Weldon Owen International, L.P.
A subsidiary of Insight Editions
PO Box 3088
San Rafael, CA 94912
www.insighteditions.com

Weldon Owen Children's Books
Creative Director: Tony Potter
Designer: Clive Savage
Editor: George Maudsley
Managing Editors: Toni Stemp and Mary Beth Garhart

Insight Editions
CEO: Raoul Goff
Senior Production Manager: Greg Steffen

ISBN: 979-8-88674-318-0

Manufactured in China by Insight Editions.
First printing, July 2025. FMG0725
10 9 8 7 6 5 4 3 2 1

ROOTS of PEACE
Insight Editions, in association with Roots of Peace, will plant two trees for each tree used in the manufacturing of this book.

FSC www.fsc.org MIX Paper | Supporting responsible forestry FSC® C207668

# Contents

The Journey Begins .......... 6
Scandinavia, 1000 .......... 10
Holy Roman Empire, 1100 .......... 16
Mongolian Plateau, 1200 .......... 20
Paris, 1300 .......... 24
Great Zimbabwe, 1400 .......... 28
Tenochtitlan, 1500 .......... 32
Mughal India, 1600 .......... 36
Beijing, 1700 .......... 40
Manchester, 1800 .......... 44
New York City, 1900 .......... 48
Sydney, 2000 .......... 52
Zed City, 2100 .......... 56
Returning Home .......... 60
Changes Through Time .......... 62
Index .......... 64

# The Journey Begins

More than a thousand years ago, a powerful group of people known as the Vikings were raiding and trading across Europe. But back home in Scandinavia, these people mostly lived a quiet life, farming and living together in villages.

Siblings Sigrid and Erik live in such a village. Like all Viking children, they spend their day doing grown-up chores. And, like all children, they get bored and go off searching for fun.

As they wander into the woods for a game of knucklebones, they find an ancient stone carved with symbols. The symbols are runes from the Viking alphabet. A memorial to a dead person is written on the stone.

## Finding the Stones

"I wish we could just get away," Sigrid grumbles. "Go to a place where children don't have to deal with the stuff we do! Adults should just let us be children and have fun."

Erik picks at a crack between two runes. Two round chips of stone fall out. Each has a rune carved into it.

"Erik! You know it's rumored those stones are magic. Anyone harming them can be cursed!" his sister says, chiding him.

"As guardian of my ancestor's runestone, I can tell you that's not quite right," croaks a voice.

## Meeting the Guardian

An old woman smiles kindly as she approaches the startled children. "How would you like to find out if that ancient magic is real," she asks, "and learn how different your lives could be?"

Sigrid and Erik nod at each other excitedly, their imaginations filled with the possibility of adventure.

"These stones you've broken off contain a powerful magic. Rub them together and you'll leap into the future a hundred years at a time."

### *Awakening the Magic*

Sigrid and Erik have picked up two stones chipped from a very special ancient runestone.

For when the rune on each of these little stones is rubbed, it awakens magic! Each rune stands for a unique magical ability—one represents time, and one space.

Rubbing both stones together will combine their magic and send the children on an extraordinary journey to different times and places, one hundred years at a time!

## A Glimpse of Magic

The children gaze at the stones now in Erik's hand. What will these mysterious objects show them?

"I will watch over you, should you choose to go on this journey," continues the old woman. When they look back up, the guardian of the runestone has vanished.

The stones feel warm and are unexpectedly heavy. Sigrid runs her finger over the markings. Each has its own meaning. One is carved with the rune ᛆ, *ár*, and the other with ᚱ, *raido*. *Ár* means plenty or year, and *raido* is a ride or journey.

As Erik's hand brushes the tops of the stones, it seems as though they briefly start glowing!

### *Spot the Time Travelers*

Travel alongside Sigrid and Erik as they leap forward a hundred years at a time! See the children explore what to them are strange new lands and cultures. Some of these might be familiar to you.

Spot Sigrid and Erik as you read through the book. Journey with them through each century as they try to stay out of sight.

Perhaps together you can find a friendly face who will help them get home to the year 1000 safely.

The children look at each other. What *was* that, and what exactly do the stones do? Before they have a chance to find the old lady to ask her, they hear their names called from the village.

## Return to the Village

The Sun is starting to go down, so they had better return. Viking children usually go to sleep when it gets dark, so the pair need to hurry to make it back in time. Sigrid grabs the stones. As they rub together again, she is sure the ground beneath them wobbles.

What will happen if they rub them properly? What exactly is it about the world they'd see? Sigrid stuffs the stones in a pouch. Perhaps tomorrow they would find out.

# Scandinavia, 1000

Sigrid and Erik get up with the sunrise for a day of chores, taking the strange stones they have found with them. While the Vikings are known as travelers and raiders, most do not spend their time on longships or in military camps. Instead, Viking children live with their families on land that is good for farming. Often, other families live alongside them in clusters that form a small settlement. Their parents work on the land and raise livestock in much the same way as the people the Vikings raid.

Living close together in sometimes remote villages offers people order and safety.

### Getting Around

People travel on horses and carry their goods in carts and wagons. Tracks pass through forests and mountains, but it is often quicker to use a boat if possible. In snowy winters, people journey cross-country on skis or skates.

## Life for Children

Viking children do not go to school. They enjoy games, but most of their time is spent doing useful jobs, such as finding berries and fruit, gathering firewood and tending the fire, and caring for animals. These tasks prepare them for adult life.

1000 — 1100 — 1200 — 1300 — 1400 — 1500

### Crops

Farmers grow vegetables such as leeks and cabbages, along with oats, rye, and barley for bread. Men handle heavier tasks while women milk animals, make cheese, and look after the gardens. Everyone lends a hand with sowing and harvesting, including children.

### Longship

The Vikings use longships for raiding and exploring. They can sail on open ocean or on shallow rivers using oars. The Vikings often raid in Britain and France.

### Waterways

Vikings often settle by fjords, inlets, or rivers. These are ideal bases for trading, raiding, and transporting goods.

### Clothes

Females wear a headscarf, a linen underdress, and a woolen overdress. Males wear woolen tunics and trousers. They grow beards and keep their hair long.

## Longhouse

Vikings live in homes called longhouses. These are built of timber, mud, and thatch or, in some areas, stone and turf. Farm animals share the building with people or sometimes have their own sheds.

1600 1700 1800 1900 2000 2100

## Inside the Viking Home

After a long, tiring day helping around the village, Sigrid and Erik head inside. Sigrid grips the stones in her hand. The Viking home, or longhouse, is a hall-sized single living room. It is centered around a long fireplace, but without windows the room is quite dark and can become smoky inside. People sleep on rugs or ledges around the edge of the room, kept comfortable with cushions and mattresses stuffed with feathers. Only wealthy people have wooden beds and furniture.

**Woman of the House**

When men are away on voyages, an important woman will run the farm and household. Nobody dares argue with her!

**Loom**

Girls learn how to spin yarn from woolen fibers and dye it bright colors. The loom is an upright wooden frame used for weaving cloth.

**Earth Floor**

The floor is made of packed earth and ashes from the hearth, and covered in places with flat stones.

## Living in a Longhouse

Life in a longhouse is very active. There is plenty of work to do, from sweeping the floor to gathering ingredients for cooking over the fire. The house is always full, as it is usually home to many people, often several generations of an extended family.

## Woodcraft

The Vikings are skilled woodworkers. They construct houses and boats from oak, pine, and birch.

Smoke from the hearth leaves the longhouse through holes in the roof.

## Animals

Livestock are sometimes kept inside at one end of the longhouse!

## Hearth

At the center of the longhouse is a firepit, which burns logs or peat. It is surrounded by stones to form a hearth, over which Scandinavians' two meals a day are cooked—one in the morning and one in the evening. The fire is the source of warmth and comfort in a Viking home.

The fire is always burning, so it is important there is always someone to tend it.

### *Time Travel!*

The children have barely walked more than a couple of steps into the longhouse when Sigrid accidentally rubs the stones together. . . .

One moment, Sigrid and Erik are walking through the longhouse. The next, everything blurs. The ground seems to shift beneath their feet, and they sense they are moving over a vast distance. What is happening?! Is this the magic the old woman spoke of? Where might they be going?

Sigrid and Erik are lost in time! Each time they use the stones, they are magically transported into the future. Where will they end up? They never know. Only once they have discovered everything they can about what life is like in each era will they be ready to return home.

# Holy Roman Empire, 1100

The ground steadies under Sigrid's and Erik's feet. They are in a very strange place. Where is their village? They both stare at the stones in shock. *Clang! Clang!* A smith is hammering away, shaping a horseshoe. A girl is herding goats. But where on earth are they? These lands are a part of the Kingdom of Germany, which together with the kingdoms of Italy and Burgundy, make up what is later named the Holy Roman Empire. They are ruled over by an emperor, who is crowned in Rome by the Pope, the leader of the Catholic Church.

**Travel**

Roads are muddy and rutted. Wagons are uncomfortable and travel is slow.

**Serfs**

Not everyone in the Holy Roman Empire is truly free. Farm workers are called serfs and are not allowed to leave their land. They have to grow crops to feed the local lord in return for protection and the right to farm the land.

**Nobles**

People here live under a "feudal" system. The nobles receive land from the local ruler, swearing an oath of loyalty to him. He, in turn, promises to support the emperor.

1000 — 1100 — 1200 — 1300 — 1400 — 1500

# Castle

The Middle Ages are a time of fierce wars. Stone castles are being built across Europe to protect those who live there. The castles can be home to the local lord or used by the emperor himself.

### Housing

Villagers build timber-framed houses near the castle for safety. They can escape behind its walls if invaders come.

### Blacksmith

All medieval villages need a good blacksmith. His role is to repair horses' shoes and cart wheels.

### Men-at-Arms

Soldiers are based at the castle. They also serve the local lord when he is off fighting other lords.

Monks live and pray in monasteries. Some study and teach, while some help the poor.

### Herding Goats

Children have many responsibilities in this era. These include looking after the animals and taking them to market.

1600 1700 1800 1900 2000 2100

## Inside the Castle

The children spot an amazing building on a hill and manage to hitch a lift there on a cart. They scurry inside. This is the castle. They see all kinds of people working here. There are cooks, water carriers, cleaners, laundry maids, hunters, falconers, and armorers.

### Kitchen

The children have found the kitchen, one of the castle's most important areas. They duck out of sight before they are spotted.

### Fine Dining

Spices from lands to the east are becoming popular in Europe. They are very expensive, so only the wealthiest can afford them.

### On the Menu

The cooks are preparing a banquet for the nobles. On the menu is goose, boar, fish, pies, jellies, and fruits. Poor people have to make do with coarse rye bread, cheese, and thin broth. The nobles eat the finest white bread.

# The Great Hall

The children sneak into the great hall. They see the lord and lady of the castle and their special guests dining at their own table. People of lower ranks sit at a lower level.

### Fashion

Men wear tunics and cloaks. Women have long dresses and a veil. Wool and linen are worn by all. Only the richest nobles can afford silk.

### Power Struggles

The lord and lady argue with two of the Pope's men over dinner. Who is the most powerful person in the land, the emperor or the Pope? This quarrel can lead to wars.

Dogs are popular as both pets and working animals.

### Music

Traveling poets and musicians entertain the court with love songs.

### *Escape!*

A guest spots Erik and Sigrid and thinks they are spies. He calls the men-at-arms. Sigrid thinks quickly. Can they get away by using the stones again?

# Mongolian Plateau, 1200

The children suddenly feel a fresh wind on their faces. The stones have transported them to an open, grassy plain. Far away, they see misty mountains, and the air smells moist, as if there has just been a rare downpour of rain. This is the vast Mongolian Plateau in Asia. Here, life is based on a tribal system. The tribes are always on the move, herding their flocks of livestock to new pastures as the seasons change. They live in portable yurts, or gers, which allow their nomadic way of life. Each tribe is led by a nobleman, and together they form the fearsome Mongol armies.

### Ger

Home is a round tent called a ger. It is made of woolen felt stretched over a wooden framework. The ger's design means it can be taken down easily so families can move to a new location.

### On the Move

When the camp moves on, the ger is packed onto an oxcart or the back of a camel, along with pots, pans, and stoves. Three or four family groups might travel together.

Small trenches are dug around the yurts so that rainwater from summer downpours does not enter the tent.

1000 — 1100 — **1200** — 1300 — 1400 — 1500

# Harsh Land

The Mongolian Plateau, a region of the Central Asian plains, is a harsh, remote place. The summer brings burning heat and the winter bitter cold. The tribes living there do not have it easy as they travel, or migrate, across an endless grassy landscape, often facing windy, exposed conditions.

### Nomadic Life

The Mongols are nomads—they move location a few times a year to find new places for their flocks of sheep, goats, cows, camels, yaks, and horses to graze. People rely on their animals for the meat and dairy products they provide.

A ger's sides can be rolled up in summer to keep it cool.

### Inside a Ger

The ger offers a warm, cozy place to cook, eat, and sleep. The items in the ger are all arranged carefully, in keeping with local customs. Family members and guests have specific places to sit.

### Life for Children

Life is tough for Mongolian children. They are taught survival skills, such as how to collect dry animal dung for fuel, milk cattle, use a bow and arrow, and cook and sew. They also learn to handle horses at a very young age.

1600 1700 1800 1900 2000 2100

## Meeting the Leader

Sigrid and Erik see an important-looking person ride into camp. They walk over to hear what he has to say.

### Trade

Merchants bring silk and tea from China to buy Mongolian fur and horses. Over time, the Mongolians' military strength allows them to build a great empire. As it grows, it encourages trade along the Silk Road, a network of routes between China and Europe.

### Horses

The horses here are stocky and hardy. They are vital to Mongolian culture. A milder climate has improved the grazing and led to a rapid rise in the number of horses, helping increase Mongolian military power.

### Going to War

Mongol warriors fight with deadly bows and arrows. Their swords are slightly curved and designed to be used on horseback. They wear helmets and armor made of leather and iron.

### The Leader

Each tribe has a nobleman as leader. He is mostly a warrior and is responsible for keeping his people safe. He also settles disputes and keeps law and order. This leader has given his allegiance to a warrior called Temujin, who will become known as Genghis Khan.

## Horse Racing

The Mongols race their horses at full gallop across the grassy plains. This exercises the horses and allows warriors to practice their riding skills. In warfare, horses can gallop for over six miles without stopping. Each warrior brings several horses to a battle so a fresh mount is always available.

## A Sporting People

Popular Mongol sports include archery and a kind of wrestllng called *bökh*.

## Food and Drink

Livestock provide Mongolians with meat, yogurt, cheese, and milk. People also gather wild plants and hunt using birds of prey.

## Clothes

Mongol men and women wear a wraparound tunic called a *deel*, felt hats and jackets, and long robes. These are ideal for the harsh climate.

## *Rub the Stones!*

There is a sense of unrest in the camp. The children feel uneasy. Erik takes the stones from Sigrid and rubs them together.

# Paris, 1300

Erik and Sigrid leap forward another hundred years. They gaze in awe at a huge settlement built along the banks of a big river. They have never seen a city before. This is Paris, the capital of France. It is one of the busiest cities in Europe and has grown to become a center for trade, politics, religion, and culture in the region.

**The Castle**

The Louvre Castle is much grander than the last castle Sigrid and Erik saw. It is built against the city walls and, with its defensive towers and narrow gates, protects Paris from attack.

**Royal Palaces**

France is ruled by a king. The royal palaces and halls are on this island. The bridges to it are defended by small forts.

**Boats Afloat**

The river is full of boats. Some are fishing boats and ferries. Others carry barrels of wine, stone for building, grain for millers, firewood, or coal.

**University**

Paris is a center of learning. Students travel here from all over Europe. Some of them study at a college called the Sorbonne, part of the University of Paris.

## Wind Power

Windmills are being built across Europe to grind grain to make flour. They are placed on high ground to catch the breeze.

## Markets

Busy markets sell cloth, grain, and much more. Merchants are becoming very rich and powerful.

## The Cathedral Age

Buildings on a scale not seen before are going up across Europe to display the Church's power and riches. They are known as cathedrals, and there is one in Paris called Notre-Dame de Paris, "Our Lady of Paris."

## Waterwheels

River currents power wheels moored under a bridge, driving mills for grinding grain.

## Notre-Dame

The children are intrigued by a huge building across the river. They cross a bridge and enter the great church of Notre-Dame.

### Stained Glass

Glass for the window is made from a mix of sand, lime, and soda ash. It is colored with metallic powders, and each pane is carefully fitted into the lead framework piece by piece.

### Building Work

Notre-Dame is itself a traveler through time. By 1300, builders have been working on it for 137 years already—and it is still not quite finished!

### Singing in the Choir

A singer sits in the choir stalls to prepare for a service. He will be joined by others, and soon their singing will fill the air. Notre-Dame is a great center of religious music.

### Arts and Crafts

A stonemason is carving a limestone column. It takes many skilled craftspeople to create a new cathedral—carpenters, wood-carvers, sculptors, artists, goldsmiths, jewelers, and bell-makers.

**Candles**

Candles are being lit. They are made of sweet-smelling beeswax.

**Christian Clergy**

In times of trouble, people turn to the Church for food and shelter. They pay the priests to say prayers for them. The priests and bishops represent the Catholic Church in Rome.

***Off Again!***

Erik is so dazzled by the beautiful colors of the great round window, he unintentionally rubs the magic stones together! Where to this time?

# Great Zimbabwe, 1400

After the cool cathedral interior, the children are hit by the heat of a blazing sun. A grassy land lies before them. Monkeys leap through the trees. They have arrived in the city of Great Zimbabwe, the capital of the powerful Kingdom of Zimbabwe in southern Africa. Its 10,000 inhabitants belong to the Karanga, a branch of the Shona people. The kingdom is at the peak of its power. It is the strongest culture in the region and stays in power by receiving taxes from conquered local rulers.

### Housing

Most of the kingdom's subjects live in houses made of wooden frames covered in dried mud. Stone buildings are built around houses for important people and officials.

### Great Enclosure

The city has several important sites, but the Great Enclosure is at its heart. The stones of its high walls are fitted together without need for mortar. It is the royal family's home and is a space for religious rituals.

1000 1100 1200 1300 1400 1500

### Crops and Animals
Growing hardy crops, such as black-eyed peas, sorghum, and millet, and raising cattle are the origins of much of the kingdom's wealth. As a result, the ruling class controls much of this trade and even manages the cattle's seasonal movements.

### Children at Work
Young people help with the important job of herding cattle.

### Metalworking
Clay furnaces are operated by skilled metalworkers. They work with iron ore, copper, and gold. Gold is one of the sources of the kingdom's riches.

### Pottery
Skillful men and women make much of the pottery needed for daily life in the city. It is used for cooking, storing food, and decoration.

### Long-Distance Trade
Great Zimbabwe lies between many gold mines and the Swahili coast of East Africa. That places it on an important trading route, so merchant expeditions are a frequent sight here.

1600 — 1700 — 1800 — 1900 — 2000 — 2100

## Inside the Enclosure

Sigrid and Erik follow the merchants. The children hide behind a wall to see more.

### Conical Towers

The big conical towers are granaries. They store grain supplies in case of drought. Their dominant position also shows off the ruler's power and importance.

## Kingdom's Center

The Great Enclosure is the center of the city of Great Zimbabwe and the kingdom. From here, the king rules land covering almost 20,000 square miles.

### Zimbabwe Birds

Statues of eagles are displayed on walls and pillars. They are carved from the soft rock soapstone. They might be tribal symbols, linked to the god Mwari.

## Royal Residence

The Great Enclosure is the home of the king and his family and is used for important activities. The king holds power through his mystical links to ancestors and his people's god.

## Trade and Conquest

Selling local products, such as gold and ivory, helps the kingdom grow and flourish. It also pays for a powerul army that has conquered neighboring kingdoms. Taxes flow from the conquered areas into Great Zimbabwe.

### *Rub the Stones!*

The children are fascinated by life in the Great Enclosure, but they want to see even more. They rub the stones to find another exciting destination.

# Tenochtitlan, 1500

The smell of cooking greets Sigrid and Erik as they land in the hustle and bustle of another city—and this one appears to be on an island in a lake! This is Lake Texcoco, and the colorful city is Tenochtitlan, capital of the Aztec Empire in what will become Mexico. In the shadow of a massive stepped pyramid are palaces, markets, ball game courts, saunas, and schools. Tenochtitlan is the most powerful of the three cities that make up the Aztec Empire.

## Aztec Empire

The Aztec Empire stretches from the Atlantic to the Pacific coasts. The conquered are not governed directly by the Aztecs but have to supply them with crops, textiles, pottery, and precious stones.

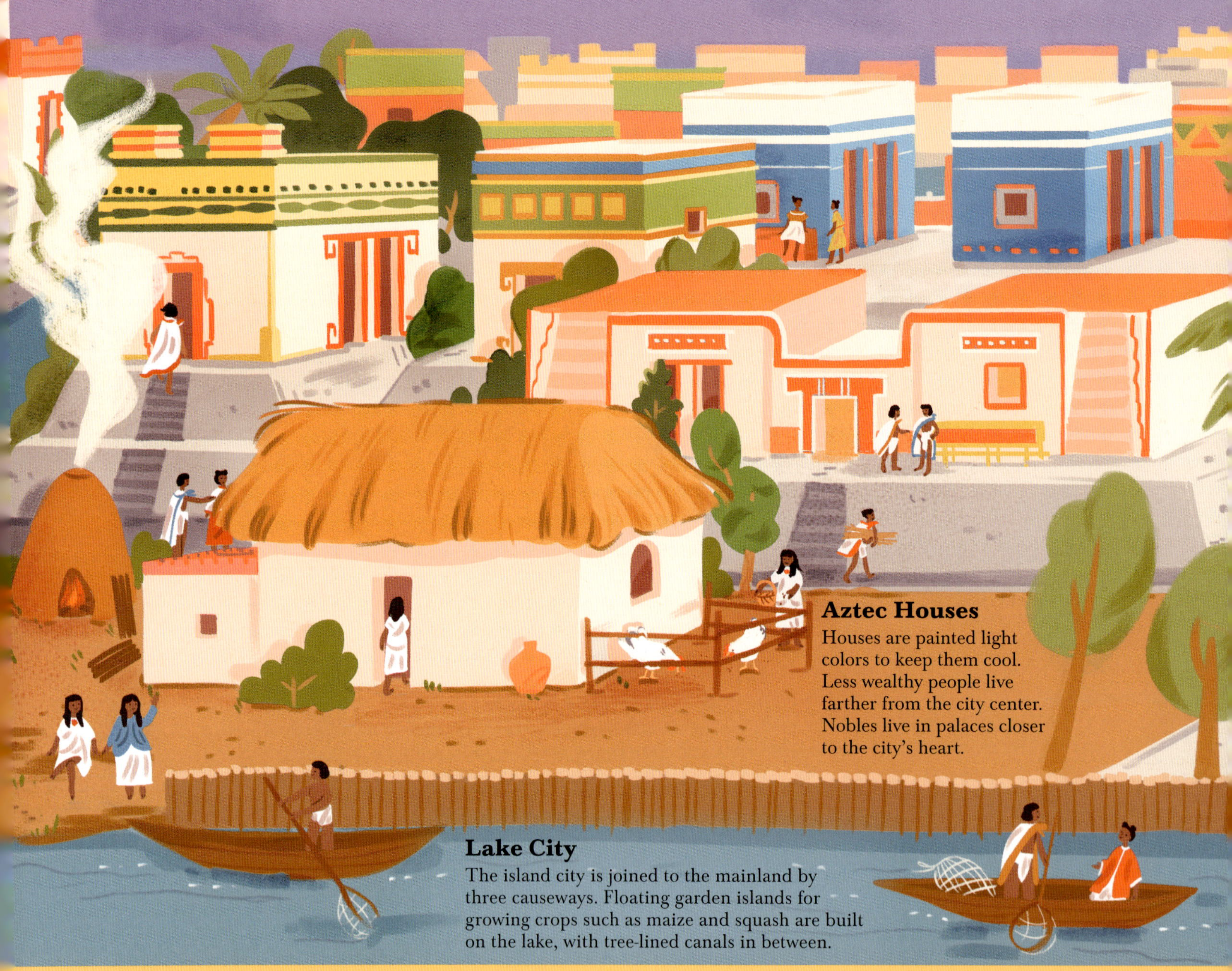

## Aztec Houses

Houses are painted light colors to keep them cool. Less wealthy people live farther from the city center. Nobles live in palaces closer to the city's heart.

## Lake City

The island city is joined to the mainland by three causeways. Floating garden islands for growing crops such as maize and squash are built on the lake, with tree-lined canals in between.

1000 1100 1200 1300 1400 1500

## The Great Temple

A stepped pyramid towers over Tenochtitlan. At the top are two shrines, honoring the god of war and the god of rain. Here, priests use people in gruesome rituals to please the gods.

The lake this city is on will one day be drained. The city that replaces it will be called Mexico City.

## Weaving Lesson

Aztec girls are taught to weave cloth from yarn made of wool, cotton, or tough plant fibers such as yucca.

## Matchmaking

Parents planning a wedding go to a matchmaker, a wise woman who will find a suitable bride for their son. They also need to check with a priest whether a marriage date is lucky or not.

## Food

People prepare food for a feast—tortilla flatbreads, avocados, tomatoes, beans, stews, fish, duck, turkey, and chili.

1600 1700 1800 1900 2000 2100

## Inside the Home

As the afternoon fades to evening, Sigrid and Erik peek inside the single room of a small Aztec house and see a marriage ceremony. The room is just for sleeping and eating. There might be a kitchen shared by other families in a courtyard outside.

### Furnishings

Furniture in an Aztec home is simple. People sleep on reed mats, clothes are kept in wooden chests, and clay pots and bowls are used for storing and eating food.

### Tying the Knot

During a marriage ceremony, the bride and groom sit on a mat in front of a matchmaker. The cape of the groom is tied in a knot to the bride's blouse to signify their new bond. Tying the knot is still a symbol of marriage in many cultures today.

### Married Life

An Aztec girl marries at about 15 years old. Much of her life will be spent weaving, cooking, and raising children. A new husband will usually be in his early twenties. He is expected to serve time as a warrior.

**Building Materials**
Poorer Aztec houses have dried mud or wood-and-plaster walls, earthen floors, and thatched roofs. Slightly wealthier houses are built of stone.

**Aztec Children**
All Aztec children are taught good manners. There are strict punishments for bad behavior. Children are expected to go to school, with noble and less wealthy children attending separate schools.

**Wedding Feast**
Huge feasts are prepared for wedding ceremonies, along with jugs of a strong drink called pulque. The partying will go on for four days. Sweet-smelling copal, or incense, is burned as an offering to the gods.

***Time to Go!***
A dog spots the children gazing at the happy ceremony and starts to bark. They had better rub the stones and leave quickly!

# Mughal India, 1600

The travelers arrive in a busy village alive with activity. Everyone seems to have a job to do. They spot a grand city on the horizon and jump on a farmer's cart heading that way. These lands are part of the Mughal Empire in India, ruled by the emperor Akbar. Under Akbar, the empire has grown to include most of India as well as many different cultures. Despite this, it is a time of stability, with Akbar's rule treating all religions equally, allowing the Muslim Mughals and his mostly Hindu subjects to live side by side peacefully.

**Village Well**

Water is fetched from the village well, a popular daily meeting place. It is vital for many village activities, from cooking to cleaning pots and washing and making clothes.

**Cotton Cloth**

Cloth is washed and dried in the sun. The empire grows a lot of cotton for textiles. Light, cool muslin cotton is popular. Indian products such as this are sold overseas, including in Europe.

1000 1100 1200 1300 1400 1500

## Villages and Cities

Most people in the empire are Hindu and live in farming villages. The empire's Mughal rulers are Muslim and live in cities. The emperor let Hindu princes keep their lands and offered nobles jobs, helping turn potential enemies into allies.

### Precious Water

Watering, or irrigation, of crops is very important in such a hot country. The Mughals have built canals and dams to control and funnel water to use on farmland.

### Tax Collector

A large part of the Mughal Empire's wealth comes from taxes on people who farm the land. Trusted local Hindus work for the emperor to collect taxes from Hindu farming villages.

### Carrying Crops

Indian villagers are very poor. They survive by growing rice, wheat, millet, and barley. Harvested crops are often carried from the fields on the head.

### Passing Trade

Roadside merchants set out their goods and their scales for weighing. They sell hot spices, spinach, mangoes, and rice.

1600 1700 1800 1900 2000 2100

## A Thriving City

Domed forts, palaces, and tombs shimmer in the heat, while walled gardens provide coolness and shade. The fine buildings combine both Islamic and Hindu traditions to create something new and unique.

### Procession

Grand processions with horses and elephants are a sight of Mughal rule. Prince Salim, heir to the throne, is visiting his father.

### Selling Fineries

Luxuries such as sweets are available to those with money in the city. These are not something poorer people can afford.

### Art

The Mughals are strong supporters of the arts and learning. The great Mughal cities of Fatephur Sikri, Delhi, and Agra are creative centers that attract painters, architects, and poets.

### Dazzling Dress

Wealthy people in the city dress very differently from poorer villagers. Ladies wear colorful silk saris or tunics, some shimmering with gold thread and embroidered patterns. Men have flared coats, trousers, and turbans. Both men and women wear ornate jewelry.

## Meeting the Emperor

The procession approaches the royal palace, where Emperor Akbar awaits his son. He is descended from the great Mongolian leader Genghis Khan—Mughal is a translation of "Mongol."

## Walled Gardens

Sections of the city are reserved for beautiful gardens where nobles can enjoy quiet and shade. Walls, trees, pools, fountains, and scented flowers and bushes are all laid out in patterns.

### *Rub the Stones!*

The city is full of excitement and color, but the children know they can't stay in one place too long. Time to explore somewhere else.

# Beijing, 1700

Sigrid and Erik rub the stones and find themselves in a very different city. It looks like a great place to explore. Over walls and roofs they catch glimpses of splendid temples, parks, and palaces. This is Beijing, and in 1700 it is the capital of the Chinese empire, in the golden age of the Qing dynasty. The Qing emperors originally came from Manchuria in northeast China and have hugely expanded the empire.

**Forbidden City**

The imperial palace buildings are the home of the emperor and the center of government. They are guarded by high walls and a great gatehouse. Commoners are not allowed in, giving it the name the Forbidden City.

**Big City**

Beijing in 1700 is a city of walls within walls, towers, and gatehouses. It is one of the most heavily populated cities in the world.

**Haircut**

Men have to wear their hair in a long braid. This Manchurian style is a sign of loyalty to the Qing rulers.

**Clothes**

Upper-class ladies dress in fine silk, satin, and fur robes. Working people wear simple tunics, loose trousers, and jackets. Some people are not allowed to wear certain clothes or colors.

1000 — 1100 — 1200 — 1300 — 1400 — 1500

### Temple of Heaven

Every year the emperor visits the Temple of Heaven to pray for a good harvest. Beijing has many temples and shrines. China has three main faiths—Taoism, Confucianism, and Buddhism.

### Flying a Kite

Chinese people of all ages enjoy leisure activities such as flying kites. These are made to flutter like butterflies or birds.

### Canals

An ancient network of waterways link the rice-growing south of the empire to the wheat-growing north.

### Tasty Food

Beijing food markets sell rice, tea, eggs, chickens, ducks, fish, and pork. Meals have been eaten with chopsticks since ancient times.

1600 — 1700 — 1800 — 1900 — 2000 — 2100

## Celebrating New Year

The children wander the city until nightfall. It is Chinese New Year, and people are welcoming the Year of the Dragon. Dragon dancers weave in and out of the streets.

### Festivals

Chinese New Year is also known as the Spring Festival. It is one of many festivals celebrated throughout the year here. Doorways and walls are decorated with paper cutouts for good luck. Beating drums and banging gongs can be heard filling the night with sound.

### Fireworks

Gunpowder and fireworks are Chinese inventions. Their loud noises and flashing lights are designed to scare away evil spirits and ghosts.

## Housing

Beijing housing in 1700 is a maze of narrow lanes and alleys, known as *hutong*. The houses do not open directly outward onto the street, but face inward around paved courtyards.

## Home Life

The head of the household is a man. He expects his family to obey him. Everyone is taught to have respect for their elders and ancestors.

### *Time to Go!*

The children are not used to the noises and flashing lights! They rub the stones to get away from the fireworks and the fearsome dragon.

# Manchester, 1800

Sigrid and Erik leave a riot of noise and color behind and arrive somewhere strikingly different. It is a dark, cloudy day. Drizzle is settling in. It is more the kind of weather that Sigrid and Erik are used to back home. Except, those clouds don't look normal—some seem to be coming from the buildings! The pair have landed in Manchester, England, in 1800. It is a time of great change in how things are made and the way people work and travel. This new way of life is beginning to spread to other countries, too. This period is known as the Industrial Revolution.

**Housing**

Many people are moving from the countryside into big cities to find work. Rows of houses—made of red brick and slate—are built for workers near factories and mines, forming large new towns.

1000 1100 1200 1300 1400 1500

# The Factory Age

Many people now work in huge new buildings called factories. Advanced machines have been invented to help build and make many things at a time, and quicker than ever before. Machines are powered by coal-fueled steam engines or water. Factories elsewhere are designed to produce pottery, textiles, glass, iron, or steel.

### Choking Smoke

Tall factory chimneys pour smoke and soot from burning coal into the air. This era sees the first widespread use of coal as a fuel. Smoke is also produced from the fires in people's homes. It can hover in a thick cloud of pollution.

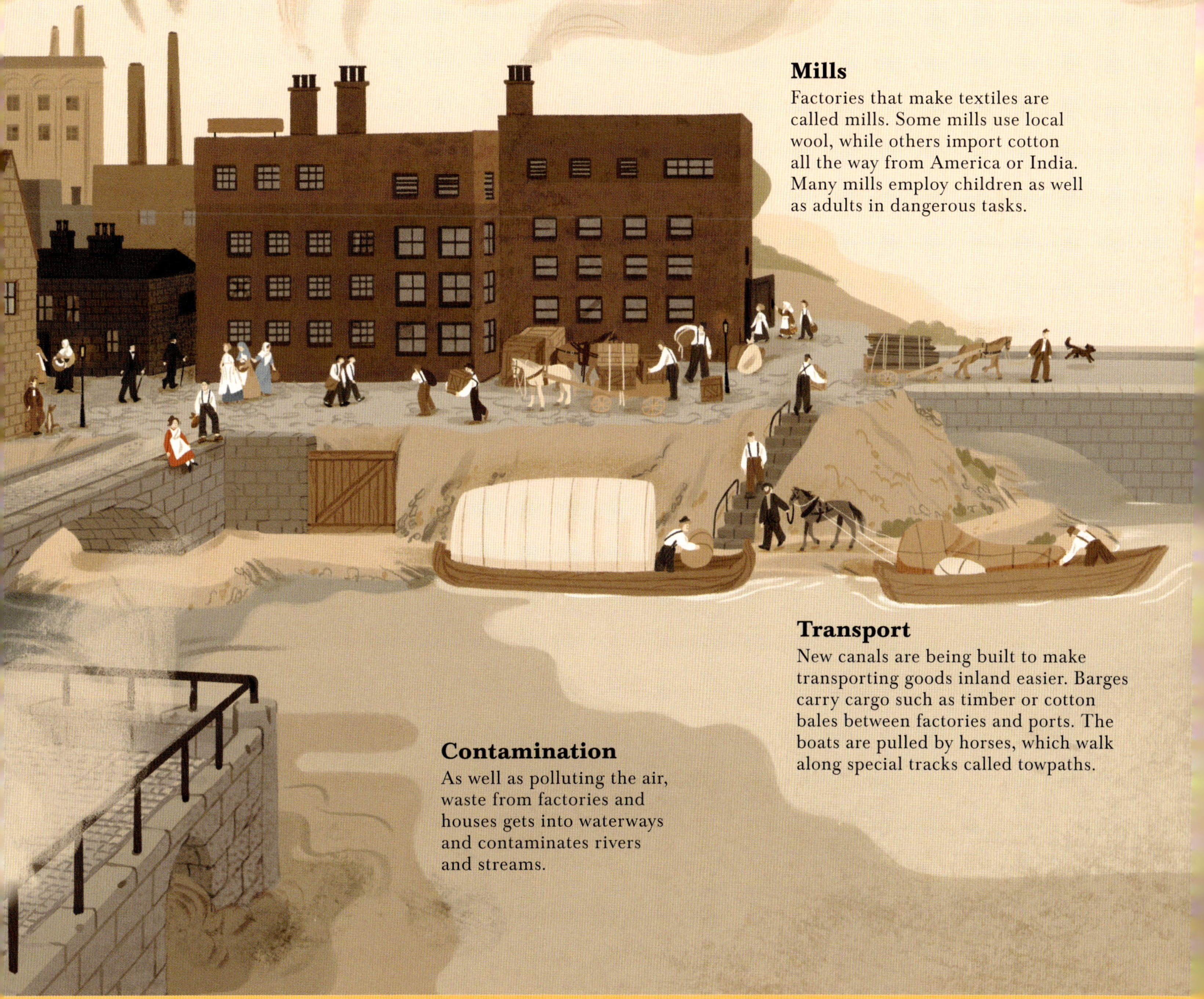

### Mills

Factories that make textiles are called mills. Some mills use local wool, while others import cotton all the way from America or India. Many mills employ children as well as adults in dangerous tasks.

### Transport

New canals are being built to make transporting goods inland easier. Barges carry cargo such as timber or cotton bales between factories and ports. The boats are pulled by horses, which walk along special tracks called towpaths.

### Contamination

As well as polluting the air, waste from factories and houses gets into waterways and contaminates rivers and streams.

1600 1700 1800 1900 2000 2100

## On the Factory Floor

Sigrid and Erik see children a similar age to them entering one of the large buildings. Intrigued, they follow them inside and onto the factory floor.

### Spinning Mule

Making thread by hand is slow. The spinning mule was a machine invented to make lots of cotton threads into yarn at the same time. This speeds the process up and creates better-quality yarn.

### Mules at Work

The machine untangles and cleans the cotton fibers. Mules roll in and out on a track to spin and twist fibers into yarn. This hugely changes how clothes are made.

Spinning mule carriages travel on a five-foot track that constantly moves in and out.

Children have to get out of the way of moving machinery before they are caught in it!

**New Technology**

Some mills are powered by waterwheels, and others by new steam engines. Power is passed to the machinery by rotating rods, wheels, and connecting belts.

**Spinning the Cotton**

Cotton fibers are unwound as the carriage rolls out. As it rolls back in, the newly spun yarn is gathered onto hundreds of long, thin sticks called spindles.

**Mill Owner**

The owner's aim is to make as many goods as he can for the lowest possible cost. His workers put in long hours, often for low wages.

**Spinner**

The person responsible for making sure the machine operates smoothly is the spinner. They need to ensure that it keeps making yarn of good quality.

**Mule Scavenger**

As the mules roll in and out, cotton fluff clogs the machinery. Small children known as scavengers squeeze under the machine to collect the fluff. It is risky work, and bad injuries are common.

***Escape!***

The mill owner thinks Sigrid and Erik are two of his workers! They rub the stones and leave before they are put to work.

# New York City, 1900

Erik and Sigrid have landed on a small island. A salty breeze blows across a harbor filled with ships. This is Ellis Island, where travelers, or migrants, are processed before crossing to New York City, the grand city across the water. Here they get their first taste of America. In 1900, ships are powered by steam engines, just one technology changing the world as machines take over many tasks once done by hand. Sigrid and Erik follow some of the migrants onto a waiting boat.

**Manhattan**
Ahead lies Manhattan, one of New York City's five districts. In 1900, New York is the second-largest city in the world after London.

**Arrivals**
Many people arrive wearing their national costumes and speaking different languages. An official checks their names and documents.

1000 1100 1200 1300 1400 1500

## An Age of Migration

People have come to Ellis Island from many lands in search of a new life and new opportunities in the United States of America. They are escaping from wars, hardship, and discrimination in their homelands. America is seen as a sanctuary offering jobs in growing industries and plenty of land.

### Statue of Liberty

One of the first sights migrants see on arrival is the Statue of Liberty, given to the US by France. It is a symbol of hope for many migrants.

### Ending the Journey

Once they have been cleared, a ship takes the migrants across to New York City. Some will make their new homes there, while others will journey on.

### Belongings

People moving to the US have brought with them everything they can carry. These are now their only possessions. Anything else had to be left behind.

## A Booming City

New York City is thriving as new inhabitants arriving from overseas help it grow. There are Italian, Jewish, Irish, and African American districts, and each has its own special character.

## Finding Work

Migrants bring their own special skills with them. They find work as tailors, cooks, carpenters, butchers, factory workers, or builders. Many are market traders, selling what they make.

### First Skyscrapers

Building technology is advancing rapidly. Some new buildings are higher than anything built before. They are known as skyscrapers. Elevators whizz people up and down their many stories.

### Steam Trains

Iron bridges with elevated tracks are built to carry steam locomotives. They link one district of the city with another.

### Streetcar

Electricity is now used to power streetcars to take people to work. This is the first era some people work in office jobs.

### Horse-Drawn Cart

Many people use horse-drawn carts to travel and transport goods. They are slow but reliable.

### Motorcar

The first motorcars are appearing. Their technology is still developing, but they will replace horse-drawn carriages.

### *Escape!*

Woah! Sigrid and Erik nearly collide with a horse-drawn cart. Better rub the stones to escape to safety!

# Sydney, 2000

The children are surprised to arrive at a much calmer place. It is a family's home. This is the edge of Sydney, Australia. The area has a lively feel because a great spectacle is taking place—the Olympic Games. For more than a hundred years, sporting competition between nations has been used to bring countries together to create a sense of unity and friendship. In 2000, technology is becoming an increasingly important part of everyday life, and people who can afford it are enjoying more leisure time than ever before.

## Lifestyle

Many homes are now built so families can spend much of their time in them. They are no longer only for sleeping and storing a few possessions but are heated or air-conditioned places of relaxation.

## Television

Pictures can not only be captured—they now move, too! The television is in nearly every home, bringing news and entertainment. Families gather to watch favorite shows, where once they would have sat together round a hearth.

## Home Comforts

Houses are now bigger and designed for comfort. Whole rooms are given to single activities, such as cooking, sleeping, washing, or sitting. Technology, including ovens, stoves, and fridges, makes people's lives easier than ever before.

1000 — 1100 — 1200 — 1300 — 1400 — 1500

### City Centers
Cities have expanded as people moved out of the centers to find more space. City centers are now places where people work and shop. Fast transport networks help people get about.

### Laptop
Computers are used for work and study. The internet enters the home for the first time.

### Leisure Time
People no longer have to work six or seven days a week. Instead, they can enjoy weekends in any way they want!

### Family
In many parts of the world, families have become smaller. Relations no longer stay in the same house or even town. Friends and neighbors instead form part of their new community.

## Schoolchildren

Children coming from the station are wearing their school uniform. Most children around the world now go to school.

## A Great Race

The cycling section of the triathlon is taking place by the Sydney Opera House, beside the harbor.

### Air Travel

Transport is now so advanced that people can travel through the skies! Plane technology allows long-distance travel, which has become more affordable. Many can now travel as tourists, just for fun.

### Organized Sport

The Olympics dates back 2,776 years to Greece, when the first ancient Games were held. By 2000, competition between teams, clubs, franchises, and countries is carefully organized into leagues, tournaments, and events.

### Holiday Time

Workers in many countries are now able to take time off work for holidays. Many people have done so to watch the Olympics.

### *Time to Go!*

The children are getting lost among the spectators! They rub the stones to take another leap into the future.

# Zed City, 2100

The time travelers arrive in the strangest place yet. By now, they are used to cities, which seem to get bigger and busier, but this one is different from the others. Huge, thin buildings scrape the sky. Many are covered in green plants. The world's population in 2100 has peaked at 10 billion people. It is a warmer place, and the weather is more unpredictable. People in this century have developed advanced technology to solve complex problems, colonize the Moon, and live longer lives.

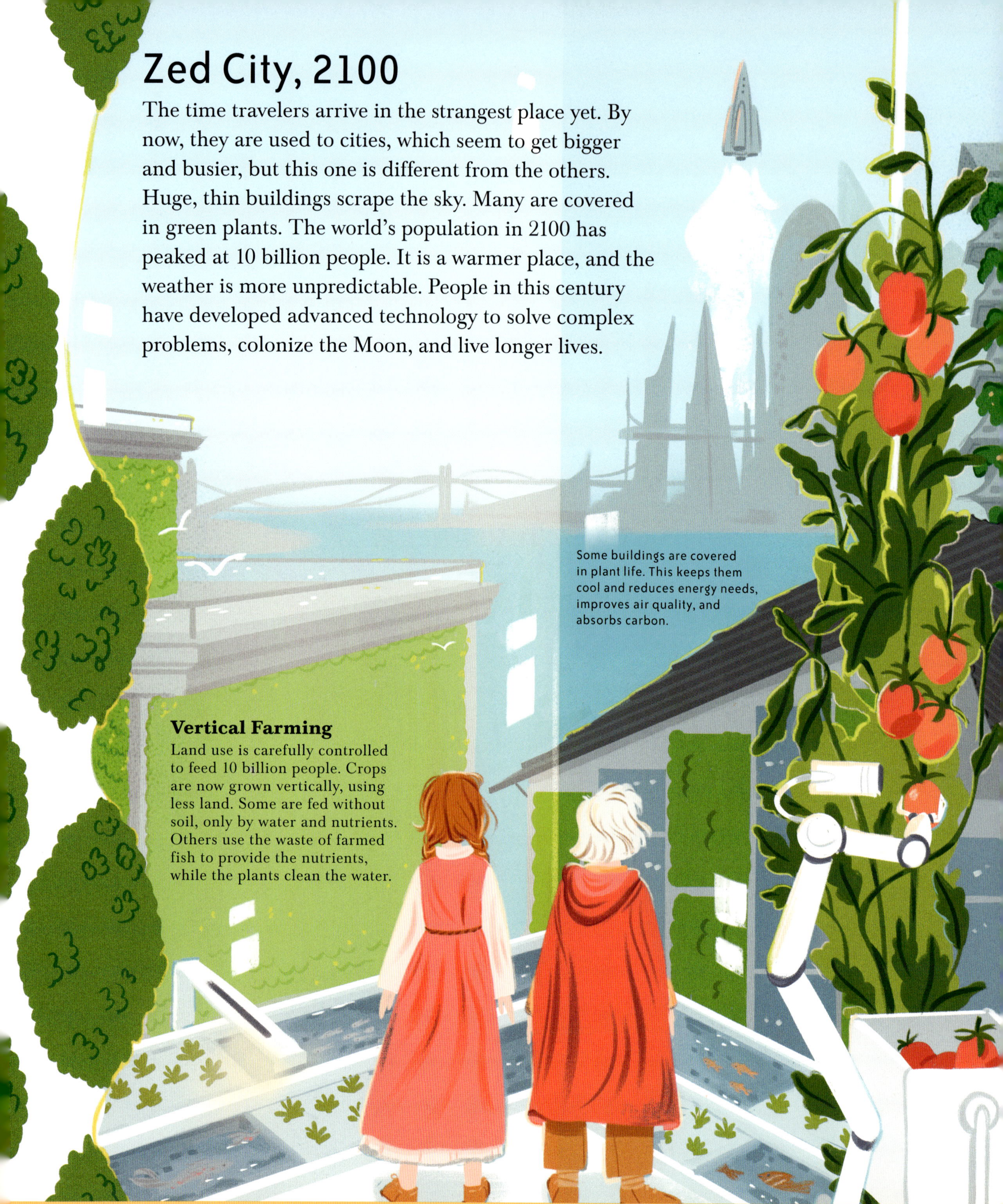

Some buildings are covered in plant life. This keeps them cool and reduces energy needs, improves air quality, and absorbs carbon.

**Vertical Farming**

Land use is carefully controlled to feed 10 billion people. Crops are now grown vertically, using less land. Some are fed without soil, only by water and nutrients. Others use the waste of farmed fish to provide the nutrients, while the plants clean the water.

1000 1100 1200 1300 1400 1500

# A Changed World

Climate change over the previous two centuries has warmed the world by 2100. Most places are affected by extreme weather, and storms, floods, droughts, and wildfires are more frequent. Rising seas have flooded some coastal areas, causing people to migrate elsewhere.

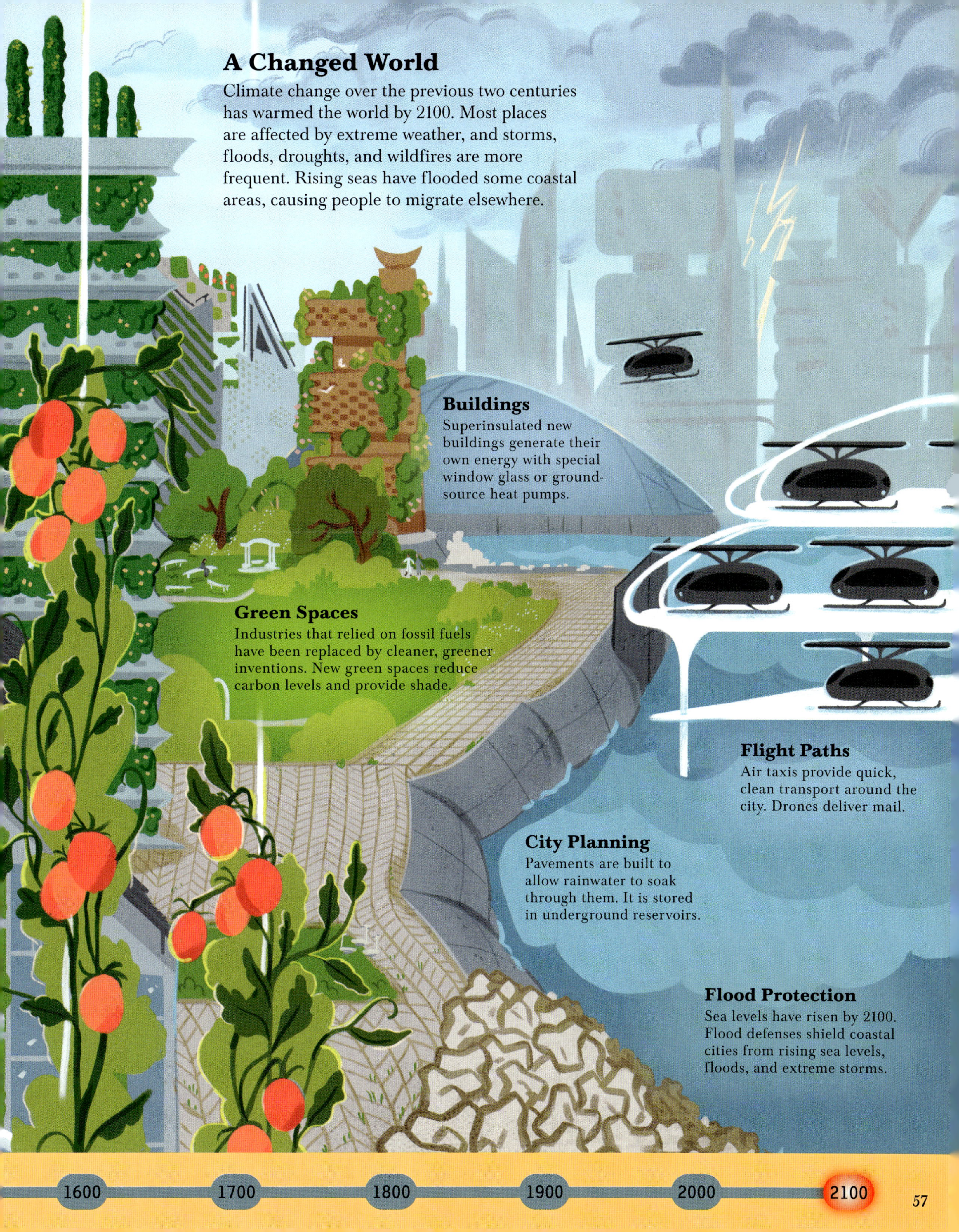


### Buildings

Superinsulated new buildings generate their own energy with special window glass or ground-source heat pumps.

### Green Spaces

Industries that relied on fossil fuels have been replaced by cleaner, greener inventions. New green spaces reduce carbon levels and provide shade.

### Flight Paths

Air taxis provide quick, clean transport around the city. Drones deliver mail.

### City Planning

Pavements are built to allow rainwater to soak through them. It is stored in underground reservoirs.

### Flood Protection

Sea levels have risen by 2100. Flood defenses shield coastal cities from rising sea levels, floods, and extreme storms.

## In the Mall

Whether in public or the home, the use of technology is everywhere. It makes life easier for people and provides more opportunities and experiences than ever before.

### Artificial Intelligence

AI is a part of everyday life. It is used to place orders and respond to questions. It helps diagnose illnesses, personalize education, and free up workers to do other tasks.

### Robotics

AI-powered robots perform everyday chores instead of humans. Others carry out surgery in hospitals, work physical jobs in warehouses, or explore dangerous parts of the world. Some even look like humans and provide companionship!

### Eating Out

Farming has moved away from raising animals for meat to be more vegetable based. Some meat is grown from cells in labs. Tiny organisms such as bacteria are scientifically changed to produce food ingredients. Also on the menu? Insects, seaweed, and algae.

## Virtual Reality

With perfectly lifelike graphics, virtual reality allows people from opposite sides of the world to interact as if they are together. It is used for entertainment, education, work, and communication.

## Space Tourism

There is a regular shuttle service to a space station on the Moon for those who can afford it. Scientists even live there permanently.

## The Latest Fashion

Lifelike holograms model the latest fashions on the catwalk. At the push of a button, you can match your size to see what the outfit would look like on you.

## Self-Driving Cars

Cars no longer need a driver, so passengers can travel in comfort and complete safety without someone behind the wheel. Roads generate their own electricity from the vibrations of traffic, so cars can charge on the go.

## *Home Time!*

Erik feels a hand on his shoulder. It is the old woman from the woods. The children know they have seen enough. They are ready for her to guide them home.

# Returning Home

The children leap across time and space once more. This time, the old woman they met in the woods—the guardian of the runestone—accompanies them. Just as she promised, she has watched over them from the moment they left their village, traveling alongside them unseen.

They land outside their longhouse. A warm glow comes from within, inviting them inside. The Sun is setting—everyone has finished their work for the day and has gone in to keep warm and get ready for bed.

## Journey's End

Although almost no time has passed in their village, Sigrid and Erik are tired after journeying so far. Their minds race after all they have seen. While their experience was amazing, there were

so many things they didn't recognize about their own world. They can't help but feel grateful for their quieter, simpler life. But they still have questions.

"How did you know what those two stones would do?" Erik asks the old woman.

"My ancestor's runestone contains a powerful protective spell, and each of its runes is a part of that spell. My ancestor was a great traveler, so your magic runes represented his travels. Maybe your complaints about life here, and your chipping the runes off, meant the runestone wanted to show you something. From your faces, I can see you've learned its lessons."

The children nod, still lost in thought.

"Perhaps we'll meet again," the old woman says with a smile as she leaves. The children wave farewell. They can't help but wonder—are their adventures truly over?

# Changes Through Time

The world changed beyond recognition during the course of Sigrid and Erik's travels. Over the centuries, every aspect of life was altered, which affected where people lived, who they lived with, and what they did for work, among many other changes.

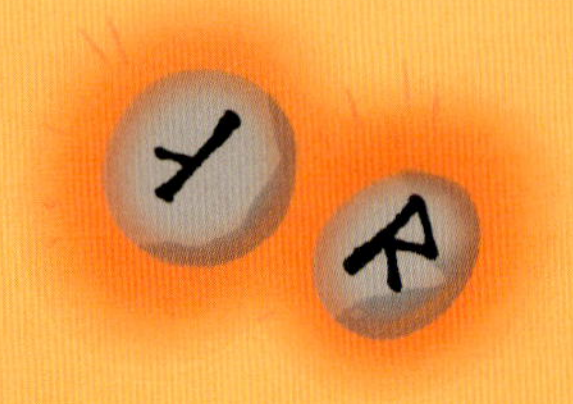

## 1100 – Holy Roman Empire

In an age of armored knights, lords build castles to protect their lands, with houses and towns growing up around them. Many people farm their lord's land as serfs but cannot leave. This is part of the feudal system, where nobles are granted land by the emperor in exchange for their service.

## 1200 – Mongolian Plateau

The Mongolians, fierce, horse-riding warriors, unite under Genghis Khan to conquer the biggest continuous land empire the world has ever known. The empire connects merchants from Europe to China along the Silk Road, allowing trade to flow across vast distances.

## 1300 – Paris

Cities such as Paris become busy centers of trade and politics, with thriving markets and new universities. Progress is later slowed by famine, war, and plague. Europe's merchants become more powerful, while the Church shows its power by building huge cathedrals, such as Notre-Dame.

## 1400 – Great Zimbabwe

Great Zimbabwe, the capital of the Kingdom of Zimbabwe, reaches the height of its power in southern Africa. Rich farmland, pottery, and gold traded with the Swahili coast of East Africa, and beyond to Persia and China, bring wealth to the nation.

## 1500 – Tenochtitlan

The Aztec Empire, and its capital of Tenochtitlan, is at its peak. The wealthy live in palaces, while the poor have only one-room dried-mud homes. The Aztecs grow food on floating islands and practice elaborate marriage ceremonies. All this is ended with the arrival of Europeans.

## 1600 – Mughal India

Much of South Asia is ruled by the Muslim Mughal emperors. They spend their wealth on great buildings, while peasant farmers pay high taxes, and offer equal rights for religions. European discoveries in science, mathematics, and astronomy this century cause people to start to view the world differently.

## 1700 – Beijing

China's Qing emperors expand their rule over a huge area of East Asia. They celebrate colorful festivals but also have rules over what people should wear. The emperor's government in Beijing rules from grand palaces that commoners are forbidden from entering.

## 1800 – Manchester

The Industrial Revolution spreads from Britain to Europe and North America. Trade, business, income, population, and cities grow as a result. European nations increase their control to rule vast areas of Africa, Asia, and Australasia.

## 1900 – New York City

New York City and the US offer new jobs for migrants fleeing poverty, discrimination, and war. The century sees the first skyscrapers, motorcars, airplanes, and moving pictures. It also sees the use of new weapons and war on a global scale. At the same time, standards of living for many improve.

## 2000 – Sydney

The home becomes a bigger and comfier living space. Rapid improvements in technology lead to various electronic devices becoming part of everyday life. The rise of and widespread use of the internet changes learning and communication. Medical care makes it possible to lead a heathier, longer life.

## 2100 – Zed City

Centuries-long use of fossil fuels to power technological growth has caused the planet to warm. The climate is less predictable. Nearly all areas of people's lives are now run or influenced by technology. People no longer have to work many jobs thanks to AI and have more leisure time than ever.

# Index


Akbar 36, 39
art 38
Aztecs 32–35
children 35
empire of 32
houses 32, 34–35
marriage 33, 34–35
Beijing 40–43
Forbidden City 40
Temple of Heaven 41
blacksmiths 17
Britain 11, 44–47
buildings 24, 28, 33, 38, 40, 45, 51, 56, 57
castles 17, 24
cathedrals 25, 26–27
houses *see* housing
children 21, 35, 46, 54
and work 17, 29, 45, 47
China 40
fashion 40
festivals 42
Qing dynasty 40
religion 41
Church, the 16, 27
clergy 27
monks 17
the Pope 16, 19
cities 24, 28, 32, 38, 40, 44, 48, 50, 53, 56, 57
climate change 45, 56, 57
clothing 11, 19, 23, 38, 40, 59
production of 36, 45, 46
craftspeople 26, 29
education 10, 24, 32, 35, 38, 54, 58, 59
electricity 51, 59
Ellis Island 48–49
factories 45, 46–47
family 10, 11, 20, 33, 43, 52, 53
farming 10, 11, 16, 29, 32, 37, 56, 58
animals 13, 17, 20, 21
feudal system 16
serfdom 16
food 18, 23, 30, 33, 37
production 25
fossil fuels 45, 57
France 11, 24–27, 49
Genghis Khan 22, 39
ger 20, 21
Great Zimbabwe 28–31
birds of 30
Great Enclosure, the 28, 30–31
Holy Roman Empire, the 16–19
emperor of 16, 17
fashion 19
housing 11, 12–13, 17, 25, 28, 32, 34–35, 43, 44, 52–53
Mongolian *see* ger
Viking *see* longhouse
India 36–39
Industrial Revolution 44–47
Karanga 28
knucklebones 6
leisure 41, 52, 53, 55
longhouse 11, 12–13
longship 10, 11
Manchester 44–47
metalworking 29
Middle Ages 16–19, 24–27
migration 20, 21, 48–49, 50, 57
Mongolian Plateau 20–23
Mongols 21, 22, 23
children 21
clothing 23
horses 22, 23
military strength 22
nomadic life 21
Mughals 36–39
architecture 38, 39
fashion 38
religion 36, 37
mule scavenger 47
music 19, 42
New York City 48–51
Manhattan 48
New York Harbor 48–49
nobility 16, 18, 19, 20, 22, 29, 32, 37
Notre-Dame de Paris 25, 26–27
Olympic Games 52, 55
Paris 24–27
pollution 45
pottery 29
religion 24, 26, 27, 30, 31, 33, 35, 41
equality of 36, 37
royalty 30, 31
rune 8
runestone 6, 7
Salim, Prince 38
Scandinavia 6, 10–13, 60–61
soldiers 17, 22
Sorbonne, the 24
spinning mule 46, 47
sport 23, 32, 52, 54, 55
Statue of Liberty 49
steam engines 45, 46, 48, 51
Sydney 52–55
tax (tribute) 28, 31, 32, 37
technology 25, 45, 46, 48, 51, 52, 56, 58–59
artificial intelligence 58
robotics 58
virtual reality 59
Tenochtitlan 32–35
tourism 55, 59
trade 18, 22, 24, 28, 29, 31, 37, 41
in cotton 36, 45
in markets 25, 32, 38, 41, 50
transport 10, 16, 20, 41, 45, 51, 53, 55, 57, 59
space travel 56, 59
United States of America 48–51
Vikings 6, 10–13
children 6, 9, 10, 12, 13
clothing 11
settlements 10, 11
women 12
warfare 22, 23, 31, 32
water power 25, 46
weaving 12, 33, 34, 47
windmills 25
woodcraft 13
work 18, 26, 29, 37, 45, 47, 50, 51, 53, 58, 59
yurt *see* ger